LEARN TO PLAY
CLASSIC ROCK PIANO
FROM THE MASTERS

BY DAVID PEARL

ISBN 978-1-4803-4127-2

HAL•LEONARD®
CORPORATION
7777 W. BLUEMOUND RD. P.O. BOX 13819 MILWAUKEE, WI 53213

Visit Hal Leonard Online at
www.halleonard.com

★ CONTENTS ★

INTRODUCTION

I've always found the best way to learn to play the piano the way my idols play is to listen to their recordings, transcribe their chords, riffs, and solos, and practice what I found. This book presents you with a mother lode of material played by an irresistible variety of rock masters, and lets you take that walk in their shoes.

As you make your way through the book, you'll explore all the different elements of rock piano technique in-depth. The book breaks down the elements that go into playing rock piano – the melodic riffs, chords, rhythms, and bass lines – and explores styles and techniques all over the map: from hard-driving rock to sweet ballads, funky blues riffs to jazz-inflected polychords.

Part I takes examples right out of dozens of famous songs from the last 50 years (and more) and shows you exactly what goes on in the piano parts. Songs by the Beatles, the Rolling Stones, Journey, Guns N' Roses, Stevie Wonder, Simon & Garfunkel, John Legend, Alicia Keys, and many more are represented here. You'll be putting your fingers on the same keys the masters played, and in so doing gain the knowledge and tools to play with confidence in your own rock band. You'll also find how the roots of rock extend back to early blues and honky-tonk and influence many of the later rock styles. Technical exercises are formed directly out of these examples, so you can isolate, practice, and incorporate the techniques into your own playing, and go further by using them in different ways in other songs, other keys, and different tempos.

Part II has seven fully transcribed piano solos by masters Keith Emerson and Bill Payne, great crossover stylists Richard Tee and Bruce Hornsby, the more recent phenom Sara Bareilles, and piano royalty Elton John and Billy Joel. These note-for-note transcriptions are written out in meticulous detail and analyzed for study and inspiration. You'll be able to look at every note in a blindingly fast Bill Payne riff, compare the ways Keith Emerson and Billy Joel build their chords, and find out how the gospel harmonies played by Richard Tee are similar to Elton John's. The accompanying analysis helps explain and distill the stylistic traits of each of these artists, from their riffs and rhythms to their triads and tremolos. Proceed and learn the way of the masters!

–David Pearl

PART I

CLASSIC STYLES AND TECHNICAL EXERCISES

★ CHAPTER 1 ★
DRIVING THE BEAT

This chapter shows you excerpts of prominent piano introductions from five songs that drive the beat forward in different ways. There are exercises leading into each excerpt to get you up to speed on the technical skills required to play them.

These five excerpts share these overall stylistic ingredients:

- A 4/4 time signature with a moderate-to-fast beat (at 90 bpm or faster)
- One part (in either the left hand or right) that establishes a steady, repeating rhythmic pattern, driving the beat-oriented pattern in quarter notes or eighth notes
- A second part that adds upbeat syncopation, working off the steady, downbeat-oriented pattern described above, and propels the beat forward in accented chord roots, reinforced with octaves
- Two-note voicings in each hand as a general rule, featuring strong, stable intervals like octaves, 4ths, and 5ths, with intervals of minor 7ths adding a bluesy color. These intervals are often reinforced with octave doubling.

ALL THE WAY FROM MEMPHIS (Mott the Hopple, 1973)

Start working on this classic rock piano song with a left-hand pattern, strong and simple, that supports the drum beat, the bass line, and outlines the two-chord progression, A7 to D, played at a driving tempo. Play along with a metronome to make sure you're keeping a steady beat, and use a fairly strong dynamic. A rock bass line like this needs to have a palpable presence.

Add a two-note-right hand part with the bottom note anchored on the note A (the common tone between the two chords) while the movement in the top note carves out a two-bar melodic hook, with an accented syncopation that drives the beat forward into bars 2 and 4. A percussive touch, as opposed to a smooth legato, is the way to go here.

Once you're comfortable playing this phrase, you'll be in good shape for most of the song. For contrast, pounding double octaves make a strong lead-in to the chorus of the song. Practice the following D major octave scale pattern, descending and ascending, to warm up:

Here is the intro to the song: 12 measures, two chords, and plenty of hard rockin'. The two-note voicing in the right hand creates an open sound, with the lower note anchoring the common tone between the two chords. Left-hand octaves are either broken or unison. The broken-octave pattern that opens the song supports both the drum beat and bass line. This builds the overall rock sound we want: a strong foundation built on low chord roots, reinforced with octaves, with a right-hand riff made of two-note intervals that emphasize the root, 5th, 7th, and 3rd of the chord. The preference for two- rather than three-note chords in the right hand is important to keep in mind, as it creates an elemental, authentic rock sound.

Energetic Rock

DON'T STOP BELIEVIN' (Journey, 1981)

In this next excerpt, the role of the main beat-keeper switches from the left to the right hand. The chord roots are still in the left hand, but here they're syncopated punches against a steady eighth-note pattern that drums out downbeat accents in the right hand. To get the hang of these, practice the following exercise, which simplifies things to focus on coordinating these cross accents.

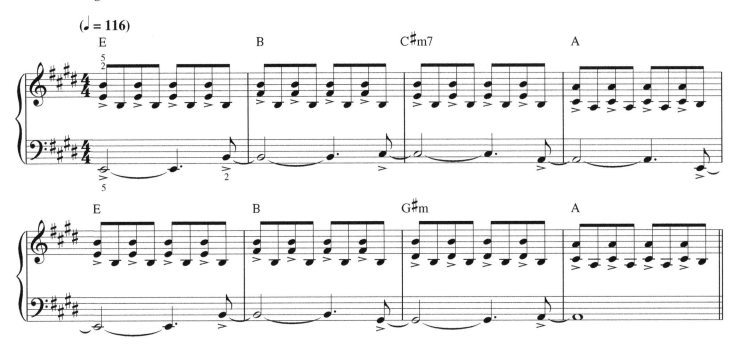

In the eight-bar intro to the song, the eighth-note oscillating pattern is combined with a bass line that's melodic and punchy at the same time, with strongly accented syncopations in the lowest register of the piano. The right-hand part features two-note intervals rather than full three-note triads, a feature shared by the previous excerpt. This open sound gives a strong tonal direction but avoids the richer sound of major and minor triads found in other styles.

LOVE SONG (Sara Bareilles, 2005)

Words and Music by Sara Bareilles
Copyright © 2006 Sony/ATV Music Publishing LLC and Tiny Bear Music
All Rights (excluding print rights) Administered by Sony/ATV Music Publishing LLC, 8 Music Square West, Nashville, TN 37203
International Copyright Secured   All Rights Reserved

This fast rock shuffle groove inverts the roles of the two hands, with the beat-keeping in the four bouncing triads in the right hand and syncopated octaves in the left.

Use the following exercise to practice this tricky syncopation. First play the two measures on the left, which are unsyncopated, then play the two measures on the right, subdividing each beat into triplets and hitting the left-hand octave on the third triplet, just before the next beat. Mastering this groove will be useful for many other songs.

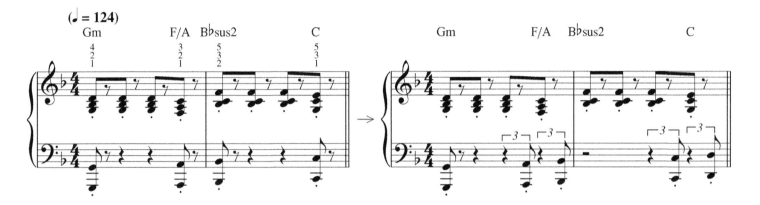

Now play the entire intro, and just remember to play the syncopated octaves in the left hand with swing eighths, as above.

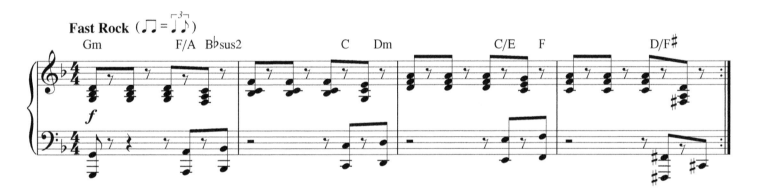

9

SHE'S A RAINBOW (Rolling Stones, 1967)

Words and Music by Mick Jagger and Keith Richards
© 1967 (Renewed) ABKCO MUSIC, INC., 85 Fifth Avenue, New York, NY 10003
All Rights Reserved   Used by Permission

Steady eighth notes in the left hand keep the beat driving forward in this next excerpt. The pattern is similar to the well-known Alberti bass, which kept the beat in the 1700s for the likes of Mozart, Haydn, and Beethoven. It worked for the Rolling Stones, too. The lower note, played on the beats, alternates between the root of an F7 chord, on beats 1 and 3, and the 3rd, on beats 2 and 4. The upper note, on all the offbeats, stays on the 7th of the chord. Keep your left hand in position to play all three notes as you gently shift the weight from the left side of your wrist to the right side. The right-hand part features an ascending scale with a slightly syncopated melody. Be sure to practice the fingering for this scale for a smooth pass-under of the thumb between the third and fourth notes. It's the syncopations that make this one of the most popular and recognized piano parts of the rock era. Bring the tempo down as you start practicing, and slowly work it up to the lively tempo of the original.

MARTHA MY DEAR (The Beatles, 1968)

Words and Music by John Lennon and Paul McCartney
Copyright © 1968 Sony/ATV Music Publishing LLC
Copyright Renewed
All Rights Administered by Sony/ATV Music Publishing LLC, 8 Music Square West, Nashville, TN 37203
International Copyright Secured   All Rights Reserved

This next piano intro has a similar quirkiness to "She's a Rainbow" and leaves an equally indelible impression. Its secret lies in the trickier syncopations in the right hand against the steady rocking of the eighth notes in the left. The useful and common left-hand pattern is grounded in a solid, four-on-the-floor beat in the lower octave. The upper octave is its rhythmic counterpart, with the higher upbeats echoing the lower and creating its own boom-chuck rhythmic underpinning.

The following exercise distills the technical necessities down into short patterns, and breaks down the syncopations into its essential components, with built-in repetitions for easy practicing.

Keeping a steady tempo with this song is paramount. Practice the left-hand part alone, with a metronome. Use a light bounce in the wrist to avoid tension and fatigue, and take breaks if your muscles start to get tight. Practice F major left-hand octave scales to prepare for the ascending octaves in measures 3 and 4.

★ CHAPTER 2 ★
BALLAD STYLE

Rock and pop ballads featuring the piano have that rare combination that draws a listener in with its opposing elements: the pairing of an aggressive sound – maybe the drums, or perhaps a distorted electric guitar – with the gently taming sound of the piano, soothing the savage beast of a love gone wrong. The most effective examples of ballad playing feature light, sustained chords or broken-chord arpeggios, rather than the full, pounding chords that drive the beat in faster, louder rock. But there is great variation in ballad style, as you'll see in the songs covered in this chapter.

Common elements you'll find in ballad playing include:
- A softer touch on the keyboard
- A spare texture (more space in between notes)
- Sustained resonance
- Slower-moving chord progressions

BREATHE (2 AM) (Anna Nalick, 2004)

This song is played with the basic elements of a ballad style: simple block chords in the right hand, only two or three notes, with a single bass note in the left hand.

The key to making the piano sound beautiful on a ballad like this is smooth movement at the keyboard. Good fingering facilitates this more than anything else. Here is an exercise that shows how you can plan out a fingering that will keep your hand position the same throughout a phrase and eliminate unnecessary movement. Once you get comfortable, begin thinking ahead to the next chord change, and mentally prepare for the fingering change, again aiming for a smooth and even transition.

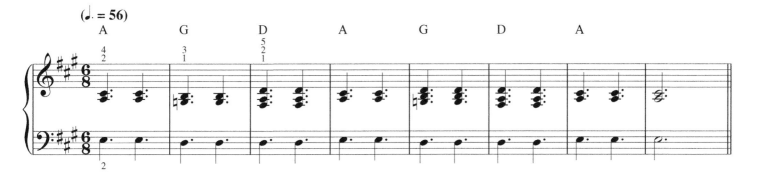

Now apply the fingering to the song, aiming for smooth transitions between chords and soft, even chords throughout.

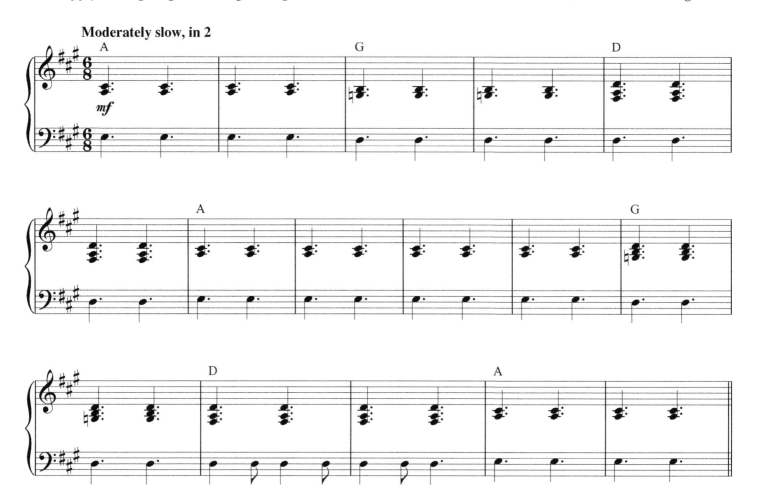

OPEN ARMS (Journey, 1981)

Words and Music by Steve Perry and Jonathan Cain
Copyright ©1981 Lacey Boulevard Music (BMI) and Weed-High Nightmare Music (BMI)
All Rights for Weed-High Nightmare Music Administered by Wixen Music Publishing Inc.
International Copyright Secured   All Rights Reserved

The next stop in a ballad style is a song with a fuller, stronger sound in the right-hand chords, supported by low-register octaves in the bass. "Open Arms" has both, along with an eighth-note triplet swing feel in 3/4 time.

To get the hang of the swing feel, practice the following exercise, first at a slow, comfortable tempo. The third note of each triplet in the left hand is where you want the swing eighth to land. You can increase the tempo up to 100 bpm, approximately where the song is played.

Mentally subdivide each beat into triplets. When you play the song excerpt, the swing-eighths will come to you easily.

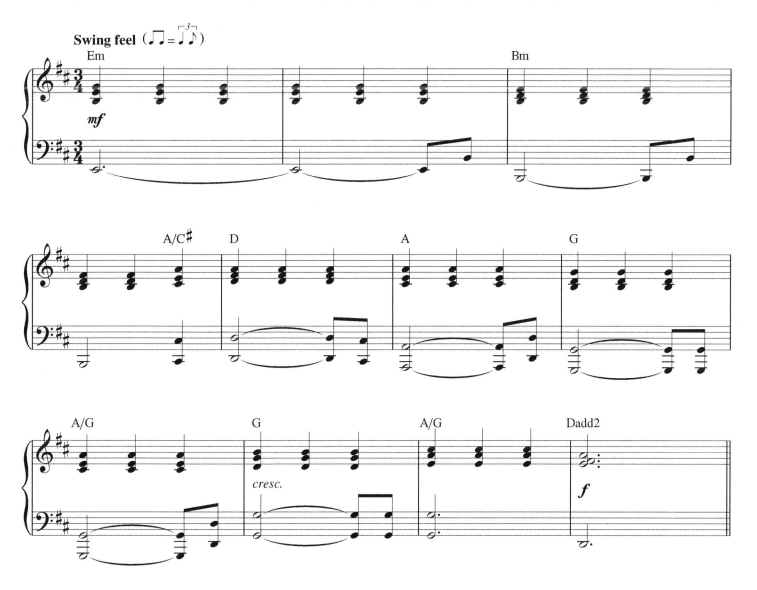

NOVEMBER RAIN (Guns N' Roses, 1991)

Words and Music by W. Axl Rose
Copyright ©1991 Guns N' Roses Music (ASCAP) and Black Frog Music (ASCAP)
All Rights for Black Frog Music in the U.S. and Canada Controlled and Administered by Universal - PolyGram International Publishing, Inc.
International Copyright Secured   All Rights Reserved

The intro to "November Rain" (see page 16) also has three-note chords in the right hand and syncopated bass notes, but adds chord extensions: 7ths and 9ths. The subtle harmonic changes here give the song interesting color and add melodic movement, perfect for setting the mood of a ballad.

As in the previous songs, the syncopated octaves in the left hand create a sense of forward movement. Here there is no swing-eighths feel – just even eighth notes, with an added rhythmic push from the two 16th notes leading into bars 4 and 5.

YOUR SONG (Elton John, 1969)

Words and Music by Elton John and Bernie Taupin
Copyright © 1969 UNIVERSAL/DICK JAMES MUSIC LTD.
Copyright Renewed
All Rights in the United States and Canada Controlled and Administered by UNIVERSAL - SONGS OF POLYGRAM INTERNATIONAL, INC.
All Rights Reserved   Used by Permission

Here the right-hand and left-hand patterns coordinate on important beats in each measure, lending the song its unique rhythmic pulse. The parts match up at three places within the measure: on the downbeat, on the "and" after 3, and on beat 4. Since the second place is syncopated and the first and third are not, a soothing, tide-like quality results from the push-pull combination.

The next exercise isolates these places so you can practice where the hands come together.

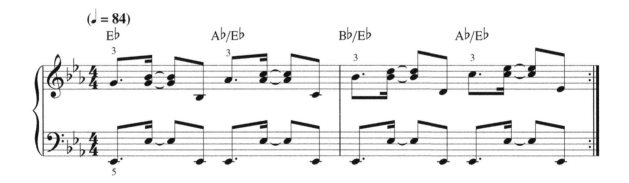

Adding the remaining notes will now complete the flowing pattern in each measure.

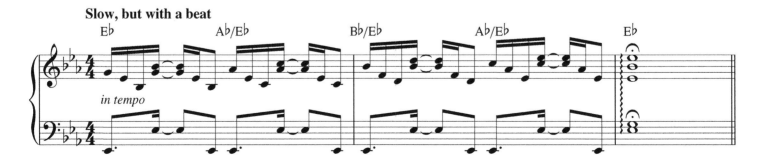

BRICK (Ben Folds, 1996)

Words and Music by Ben Folds and Darren Jessee

The intro to "Brick" features a two-measure pattern of coordinated rhythms in each of the right- and left-hand parts. Because the left-hand part is syncopated where the right hand isn't, and the right-hand part plays when the left hand doesn't, it can take some practice to develop this more intricate style.

The following exercise breaks down the patterns into components you can practice in repeated loops.

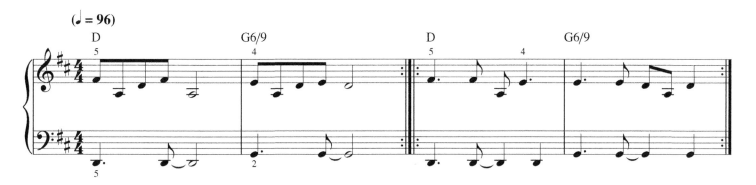

Once you feel the hand coordination coming together as a unified action, the intro will be easy to put together.

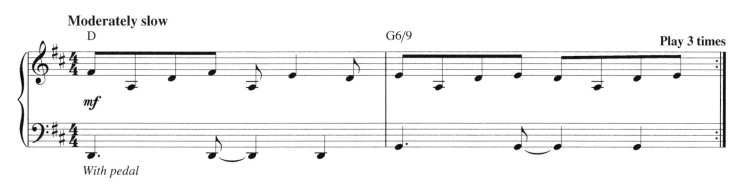

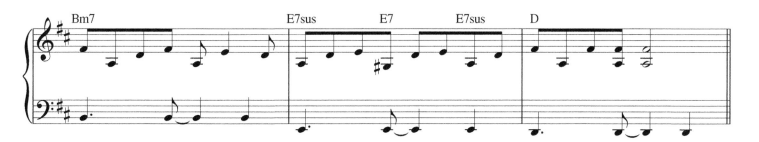

17

SUMMER, HIGHLAND FALLS (Billy Joel, 1976)

Words and Music by Billy Joel
Copyright ©1976 JOELSONGS
Copyright Renewed
All Rights Administered by ALMO MUSIC CORP.
All Rights Reserved   Used by Permission

The rippling, flowing eighth notes of this Billy Joel song are a classic example of a ballad style perfectly suited to the piano. As in Bach's famous "Prelude in C Major" from *The Well-Tempered Clavier, Book I*, the eighth notes in the right hand are derived from chord forms that are set in motion in a changing pattern of arpeggiated chord tones, with an occasional passing note added between them for melodic effect.

Because they are derived from chord forms, an excellent way to practice is to line up the eighth notes in a vertical chord to practice the individual hand positions and the movement between them. This makes it easier to see the chord progression as a whole as well as the changes from measure to measure. Practice the forms in the following etude, paying close attention to the fingering.

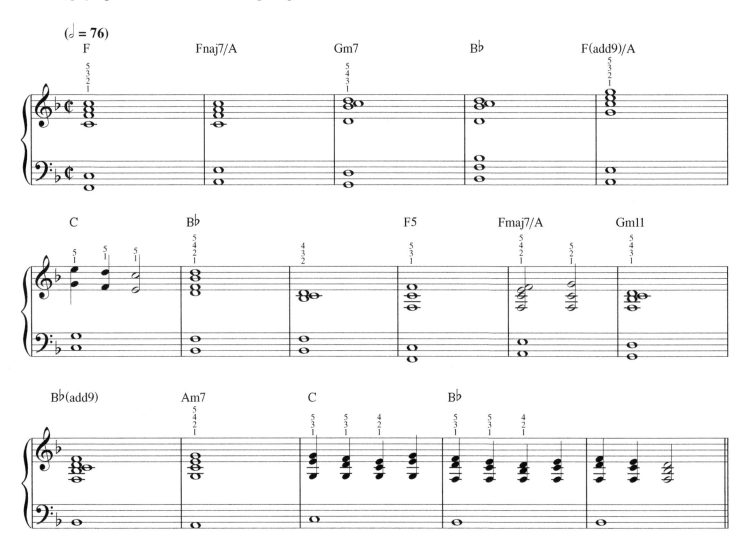

Once you can move easily and quickly from chord to chord, playing the "Summer, Highland Falls" (page 19) outro will be much easier, with your hand and fingers set in position to arpeggiate the chord notes smoothly and move to the next hand position.

HEAVEN CAN WAIT (Meat Loaf, 1977)

Words and Music by Jim Steinman
Copyright ©1977 by Edward B. Marks Music Company
Copyright Renewed
International Copyright Secured   All Rights Reserved
Used by Permission

The beautifully florid piano interlude in the middle of this song sets a dramatic example for rock ballads – replete with classical-sounding left-hand Alberti bass accompaniment and soaring melodic phrases harmonized in 3rds, 6ths, and octaves. Meeting the challenge of this rhapsodic passage requires a multi-step approach. Playing hands alone is a must at first. Plot out the fingering in the left hand before you go at it. If you don't, the fingering problems will definitely trip you up as you put the hands together.

The exercise on page 20 breaks down the difficult right-hand passages into small sections that can be repeated for accuracy and speed. It also slows them down. The sections focus on the descending 3rds and 6ths, ascending octave runs, octave chords, and the D major arpeggio that ends the interlude. Practice and repeat as you need to master the skills, then apply them in the interlude that follow.

★ CHAPTER 3 ★
GOSPEL ROCK

The piano is central to the sound of gospel music and the role it plays in church, supporting soloists and choirs by playing big, full chords in spirit-soaring grandeur.

The characteristically big-chord voicings of gospel style – reinforced with doubled notes and octaves in the bass – imitate the full, sustained sound of the church organ. Gospel style incorporates lots of harmonic interest, like the traditional "Amen" cadence (IV-I) and diatonic chord progressions, or chords built on the notes of the diatonic scale. Other hallmarks include:

- Ripple effects – arpeggios, or rolled chords
- Ascending and descending diatonic progressions with chromatic passing chords
- Left-hand octave techniques – octaves and broken octaves

LET IT BE (The Beatles, 1970)

The piano interlude in "Let It Be" features stylistically conventional church chords, played with octaves in the right hand that are filled in with one and two notes, and single notes and broken octaves in the left hand. To get your hand comfortable with the span and chord shapes, practice this exercise for right-hand octave chord technique.

The progression emphasizes the IV-I progression, giving the song its prayer-like character. The descending gesture lends a sense of calming release.

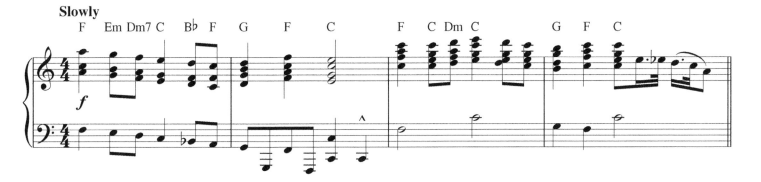

IT DON'T HAVE TO CHANGE (John Legend, 2004)

Words and Music by John Stephens and Dave Tozer
Copyright © 2004 BMG Sapphire Songs (BMI), John Legend Publishing (BMI), Sony/ATV Music Publishing LLC (BMI) and Tozertunes Publishing (BMI)
Worldwide Rights for BMG Sapphire Songs and John Legend Publishing Administered by BMG Rights Management (US) LLC
All Rights for Tozertunes Publishing Administered by Sony/ATV Music Publishing LLC, 8 Music Square West, Nashville, TN 37203
International Copyright Secured   All Rights Reserved

In John Legend's ode to the power of the family, gospel techniques are front and center from the beginning to the end. In the intro, rippling octave chords (arpeggiated, or rolled) are paired with grace note pickups in the left-hand bass notes.

To practice the rippling chord effect, try this exercise for rolled chords in the right hand. Hold down each note of the rolled chord as you play it, and listen for all four chord notes sustaining together when you reach the top note. Be aware that the top note of the chord should land on the beat when you play these rolled chords.

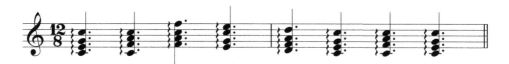

The ascending diatonic progression and the 12/8 time signature are very common in gospel style, delivering pulsing, triplet rhythms with accented backbeats.

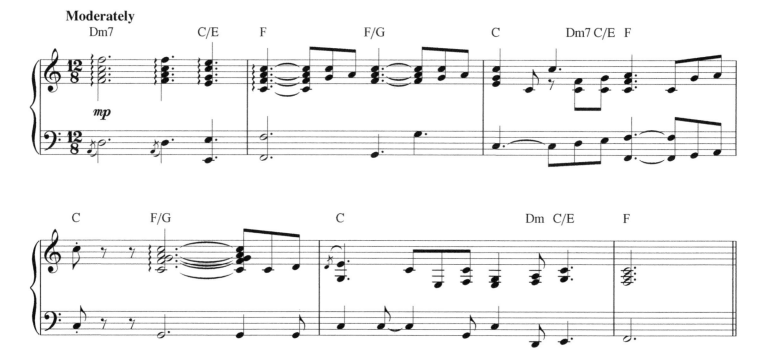

MINUTE BY MINUTE (The Doobie Brothers, 1978)

The Doobie Brothers expanded their musical horizons with the addition of Michael McDonald on vocals and keyboards in the mid-'70s. McDonald brought in church-style harmonies to the band's already eclectic rock.

One of the novel techniques used in "Minute by Minute" involves layering the tight, four-note diatonic harmonies in the right hand moving over a bass line that outlines a steady, single harmony. The other makes use of chromatic passing chords between dramatically ascending diatonic harmonies, all with a complex two-against-three feel brought on by alternating octaves in triplet rhythms in the left hand.

Play the following exercise for alternating octave triplets, and work on bringing out the tension between the octaves, grouped in twos, and cross-accents, grouped in threes.

Now add the right hand to this left-hand technique, and you ratchet up the tension with chords that reinforce the octave groupings against the triplets. You've got the famous "Minute by Minute" interlude.

GONE AT LAST (Paul Simon, 1975)

Words and Music by Paul Simon
Copyright © 1975 (Renewed) Paul Simon (BMI)
International Copyright Secured   All Rights Reserved
Reprinted by Permission of Music Sales Corporation

In gospel style, a quintessential chordal move is from a major chord to a borrowed chord and back. In "Gone at Last," the IV chord (F major) is the borrowed chord to the I chord (C major), and the motion alternates quickly from the I to the IV and back. And when the progression moves to the IV chord, the F major is treated as a kind of temporary I chord, alternating with its IV, B♭ major. Other borrowed chords to the I chord include the ii, i°, and I7. You can practice these borrowed chords in the following exercise for C major progressions.

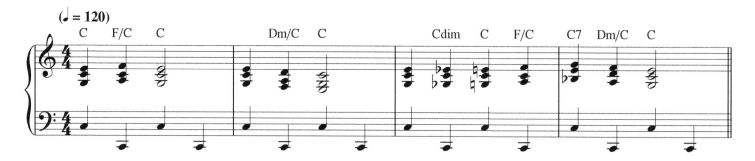

The "Gone at Last" intro (page 25) takes these borrowed chords to church with syncopation and a steady-four bass pattern in the left hand. The last two measures feature an ascending diatonic progression filled in with chromatic passing chords, making an interesting comparison to the "Minute by Minute" interlude above.

Moderately fast, with a double-time feel

BRIDGE OVER TROUBLED WATER (Simon & Garfunkel, 1970)

Words and Music by Paul Simon
Copyright © 1969 Paul Simon (BMI)
Copyright Renewed
International Copyright Secured   All Rights Reserved
Used by Permission

With one of the most well-known and revered piano parts in classic rock, "Bridge Over Troubled Water" is chock-full of classic gospel rock techniques. It has rolled chords, left-hand octaves, "Amen" cadences, and borrowed chords galore. Pianist Richard Tee brings hand-to-hand rhythmic patterns, a wealth of chord inversions, and of course the famously thundering octaves in the bass register that define the interlude and ending to the song.

To bring this style off, you need to develop a big piano sound. To that end, it's good to practice two-handed scales, with octaves and four-note octave chords in the right hand, covered in this next exercise.

You'll also need fluency with borrowed chords in E♭ major, with open-position voicings, given here in simplified form and then with Richard Tee-style rhythmic variations.

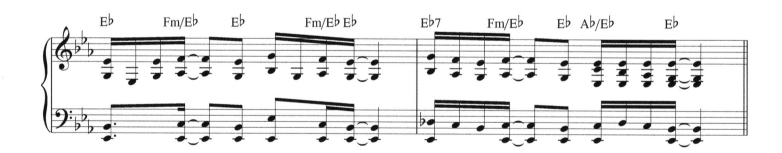

Put it all together in the interlude from "Bridge Over Troubled Water."

CHAPTER 4

BLUES AND BOOGIE ROCK

Adding some signature blues and boogie stylistic riffs can bring up the temperature of a song. Here are some of the techniques and features to look for in this style:

- The blues scale, used in melodies and riffs
- The 12-bar blues form featuring I7, IV7, and V7 chords
- Blues slides using grace notes
- Triplet rhythms

WHOLE LOTTA SHAKIN' GOIN' ON (Jerry Lee Lewis, 1957)

We start our exploration of this chapter with some common ingredients in blues and boogie: the triplet "shuffle" feel, notated here in dotted-eighth-note rhythms, and more frequently with swing eighths as in the songs later in this chapter; a bass line that "walks" quarter notes up and down chord notes or scale notes; four-note chords with the 6th added to the I chord and the 7th (as well as the occasional 9th) added to the V chord.

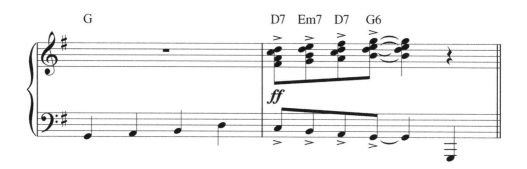

MAN OF THE HOUR (Norah Jones, 2009)

Words and Music by Norah Jones
© 2009 EMI BLACKWOOD MUSIC INC. and MUTHAJONES MUSIC LLC
All Rights Controlled and Administered by EMI BLACKWOOD MUSIC INC.
All Rights Reserved   International Copyright Secured   Used by Permission

One of the simple yet effective techniques Norah Jones uses is adding grace notes – usually a half step below the note it approaches. These are played in a relaxed manner, not fast, and legato – smoothly connected. Don't lift your finger to release the grace note until the finger that will play the main note is on its way down. Experiment with how much emphasis and time you give to the grace notes in "Man of the Hour" to see how much bluesy character you can give to the song.

Also note the open-chord voicing: two chord notes in each hand, with the root and the 5th or 7th in the left hand and the 3rd and 5th or root in the right hand. And the triplets leading chromatically down to the final chord are an excellent example of one of the most popular blues and boogie endings.

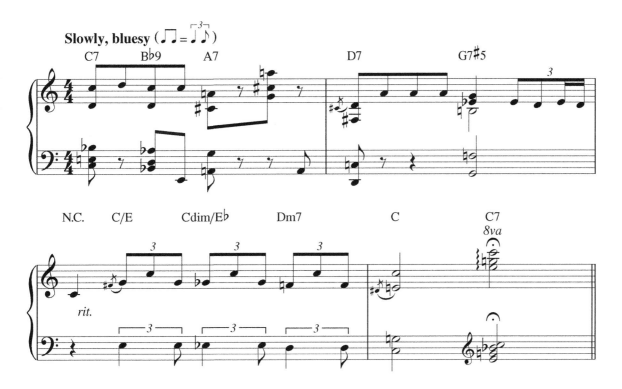

ROLL AWAY THE STONE (Leon Russell, 1970)

Words and Music by Leon Russell and Greg Dempsey
Copyright © 1970 (Renewed) by Embassy Music Corporation (BMI) and BMG Rights Management (Ireland) Ltd. (IMRO)
All Rights for BMG Rights Management (Ireland) Ltd. Administered by Chrysalis One Music
International Copyright Secured   All Rights Reserved
Reprinted by Permission

Propelled by a nonstop eighth-note rhythm, the octave eighths in the left hand of this song echo boogie-woogie piano styles, pounding out the rhythm eight to the bar. Seventh chords, grace notes, and a blues scale riffs fill out the style here. The chord progression moves from IV7 to I7, an elemental slice of the typical 12-bar blues progression. To ornament the riffs, chord notes are approached by a neighboring note either a half or whole step above or below. The grace notes are used mainly to mash together the minor and major 3rd, getting the bent-note bluesy sound. The melodic lines make good use of the blue notes, the ♭3rd, and ♭7th notes of the scale.

ROSANNA (Toto, 1982)

Words and Music by David Paich
Copyright © 1982 Hudmar Publishing Co., Inc.
All Rights Controlled and Administered by Spirit Two Music, Inc.
International Copyright Secured   All Rights Reserved

The wonderfully funky riffs in this example come from using two kinds of blues scales over a G7 chord vamp. The G pentatonic scale with the ♭3rd and 7th added is combined with a G minor blues scale, with its ♭5th giving the bluesy bite to the runs.

The exercise below gives you practice runs up and down both scales, over the same left-hand vamp used in the song.

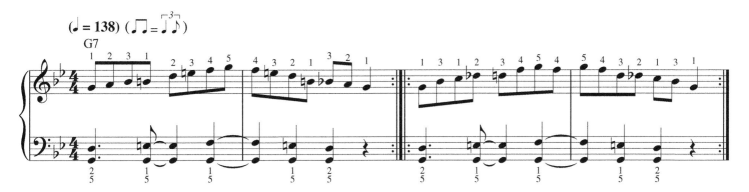

The solo on page 32 takes these scales and adds some varied articulation, grace notes, two-note shakes and accented syncopations to the mix, creating a potent cocktail of rhythm and blues.

MANDOLIN RAIN (Bruce Hornsby, 1986)

Words and Music by Bruce Hornsby and John Hornsby

This song reflects a subtler use of blues elements: the opening riff subdivided into triplet 16ths, the pentatonic scale with just a sprinkling of grace notes, a syncopated rhythm, and a chord progression that approaches the I, IV, and V chords from neighboring chords.

Built almost completely out of the G pentatonic scale, right-hand octave lines, octave chords, and triads are harmonized with notes from the diatonic scale, diatonic triads (using the Am chord to fill in the octave A-A and E-E built on the second note of the scale or Em chord to fill in the octave E-E), and open 4ths and 5ths to create a sound that recalls the four open strings of a mandolin (tuned in 5ths, as a violin, from the lowest G up to a D, then A, then E) which together make up four of the five notes in the pentatonic scale.

Single-note roots are in the bass, in the low register. In the left hand, the single-note roots of the four chords (Am7, G, Em7, D) outline notes in the pentatonic scale.

The exercise below is designed to work with the finger-busting challenges this style poses. Practice slowly at first, and increase the tempo as your chord-to-chord movement improves.

Now you'll feel more comfortable working through Hornsby's intro on page 34. The left-hand part, in contrast to the right hand, is fairly simple: single-note roots in the low register, in a one-measure rhythmic pattern that features a dotted-quarter-note syncopated figure.

★ CHAPTER 5 ★
NEW ORLEANS-INFLUENCED ROCK

New Orleans Rock developed alongside other blues styles, but features its own brand of rhythmic mojo. Marked by prominent left-hand patterns that are a fundamental component of a well-rounded rock piano technique, it has the following characteristics:

- Blues-based chord progressions using I7, IV7, and V7 chords
- Complex left-hand patterns
- Syncopated rhythms found in both triplet-based swing- and straight-eighth-note rock

NEW ORLEANS BLUES (Jelly Roll Morton, 1925)

The melodic line of this piece is built on the B♭ blues scale. The blues scale adds two notes to the pentatonic scale: the ♭3rd and the ♭7th. The next exercise shows these two scales side by side. Practice both scales with the fingering provided to develop an easy flow up and down the scales.

The left-hand part is essential to the feel of New Orleans Rock. The motion from lower bass note to upper chord originated in the stride-piano style used by blues and ragtime musicians, and typically jumped from a bass note to an upper chord, back down to a bass note to an upper chord on each beat of 4/4 time. The New Orleans version is syncopated, with the upper chord delayed half-a-beat and held over into beat 3 before returning to a bass note on beat 4. This asymmetrical stride variation gives it the kick that is as funky as it is addictive. The following exercise lets you practice the jump, starting small and working into larger jumps. Work on this left-hand technique while paying attention to the motion of your arm and hand. Try to minimize any extra movement – twisting and turning, or extending your fingers – and look to keep your hand as quiet as possible. (You can find this syncopated left-hand style in "Dixie Chicken," bars 5–12, later in this chapter.)

Now you'll find putting together these 12 bars from the opening of Jelly Roll's "New Orleans Blues" much easier.

BLUEBERRY HILL (Fats Domino, 1956)

This song features an unmistakable left-hand pattern that is based on a boogie pattern, not over a 12-bar blues progression but an eight-bar variation that starts on the IV chord. The bass line is very melodic, outlining an ascending major triad with a bluesy, added ♭3rd on beat 4.

The following exercise promotes fluency in this finger-buster. Aim to play this with a relaxed hand – if you're playing with tension, you will easily get tired and may experience muscle cramping. An easy down-up motion, with your wrist dropping down on the beats and lifting slightly on the second and third notes of the triplet, will help the rolling rhythm along.

Adding the melody in this song excerpt will be easier after playing the etude. Focus on where the notes of the melody coincide with the left-hand pattern and practice coordinating both hands.

HONKY CAT (Elton John, 1972)

The left-hand pattern in this song is simpler than some of the others in this chapter, but there is more complexity in the right-hand part. Here the melodic line is harmonized in triads and 3rds, including chromatic notes where the harmony clashes wonderfully with the underlying bass part, but only briefly, moving in passing to more consonant chords.

Play the following exercise for the right-hand chords and runs, first practicing a chromatic approach to a G major triad from a half step below and then practicing notes from a G blues scale harmonized with major and minor triads.

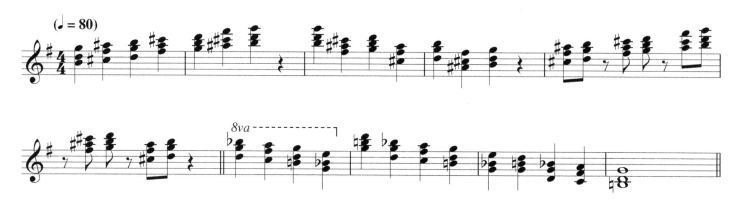

Elton John's honky-tonk style is challenging for the hand independence required. Keep a loose feeling throughout your arms and hands, and practice the coordination at slower tempos before plunging in at the desired tempo.

Moderately, in 2

DIXIE CHICKEN (Little Feat, 1973)

Words and Music by Lowell George and Martin Kibbee
Copyright © 1973 (Renewed) Naked Snake Music (ASCAP)
All Rights Reserved

This intro solo shows a wealth of blues licks over a 12-bar blues progression. The techniques are similar to those in "Mandolin Rain" (in Chapter 4), but are even more challenging with a demanding New Orleans-style syncopated-bass groove. And like the "Rosanna" solo (also in Chapter 4), the blues licks combine both major and minor 3rds, sometimes with startling juxtapositions. This time the key is A major.

Practice a few choruses of the left hand by itself before adding the right hand.

TIPITINA (Professor Longhair, 1954)

Tipitina (see page 42) may be the most challenging of these New Orleans-style pieces. The left-hand part is more difficult, covering a greater range of the keyboard and generally in a lower register. The one-measure patterns, all as evocative as they are typical, are combined here in a 12-bar blues form. The dotted-quarter rhythm that starts measure 1 and 4, the walk-up to the IV chord in measure 2, and the syncopated triad pattern starting measure 7 are all standard and recognizable blues patterns. This last is rhythmically related to Jelly Roll Morton's assymetrical stride pattern in "New Orleans Blues."

The right-hand part, heavily ornamented and riff-oriented, combines chordal motifs with open-octave lines and riffs, and chromatic neighboring notes or chromatic movement.

The following etude allows you to practice the grace notes by playing with more separation between the grace note and the chord, then moving them together. Let your ear tell you how much time and overlap you want to give these grace notes, experimenting with the amount of bluesy mash you want. The exercise works with the grace notes used in the song's main riffs.

Moderate Blues

★ CHAPTER 6 ★
JAZZ-ROCK HARMONY AND RHYTHM

The influence of jazz goes back to the early days of rock 'n' roll. Rock pioneers like Roy Orbison, Bo Didley, and Elvis Presley used 12-bar blues forms and syncopated rhythms for their '50s-era hits. Improvised sax, harmonica, and piano solos were also common features. But starting in the late 1960s, the richer harmonies of jazz found their way into the vocabulary of rock and pop, especially that of the Motown- and R&B-influenced songwriters. Several of the most important features include:

- Harmonies that colorfully highlight the upper chord extensions – the 7th, 9th, 11th, and 13th of the chord

- Lighter chord voicings

- Chromatically altered harmony, which uses notes outside the key of the song

- Complex rhythms involving triplet-based swing or syncopated 16th-note rhythms

- Jazz-inflected solo lines

ISN'T SHE LOVELY (Stevie Wonder, 1976)

Words and Music by Stevie Wonder
© 1976 (Renewed 2004) JOBETE MUSIC CO., INC. and BLACK BULL MUSIC c/o EMI APRIL MUSIC INC.
All Rights Reserved   International Copyright Secured   Used by Permission

Stevie Wonder's classic is based on a fast shuffle rhythm with a pronounced triplet subdivision of each beat. The right- and left-hand parts make use of hand-to-hand alternation of these triplet rhythms. The jazz-style chord progression makes use of 7th, 9th, and 11th chords, moving in 4ths, from the vi to the II7 to the V11 to the I. Showing a knack for jazz voice leading, Stevie includes chromatic movement of the lowest note in the right-hand part, as it resolves down from B to G♯. This movement is echoed in the triplet on beat 4, measure 4 of the left hand, descending chromatically from E to C♯.

The exercise below will help practicing the difficult "drumming" technique, where the hands alternate "strokes" of a triplet rhythm. Be sure to count each beat and its subdivision ("one-trip-let, two-trip-let, three-trip-let") either out loud or in your head.

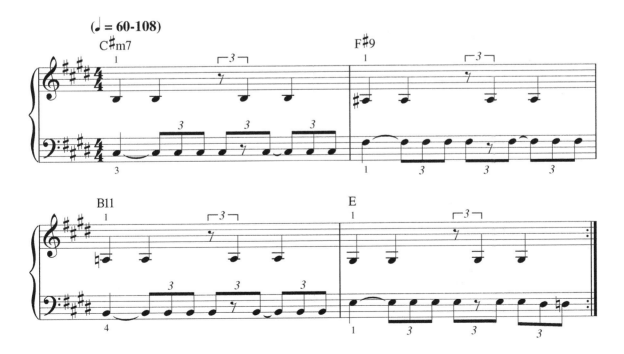

Once you feel comfortable counting the triplets throughout the measure and coordinating the hands as they alternate coming together and alternate drum strokes, moving on to the intro will be a snap.

STILL CRAZY AFTER ALL THESE YEARS (Paul Simon, 1975)

Words and Music by Paul Simon
Copyright © 1974, 1975 Paul Simon (BMI)
International Copyright Secured   All Rights Reserved
Used by Permission

This song is influenced as much by gospel as it is jazz, but the unusual chord changes show a deeper connection to jazz. These changes, loaded with jazzy 7ths, 9ths, and 13ths, are numerous in comparison with most gospel and rock harmony, and the triplet swing rhythm also shows the influence of jazz. The anticipations, like the one on beat 3 of the first measure, and the many chromatically altered leading tones (e.g., measures 7 and 8) that strengthen the push-pull dynamic of the harmony are also noteworthy.

Other signs of jazz influence are in the resolution to the relative minor in measure 15 and to an unresolved I chord in measure 19, where the notes of the G9 delay a resolution to the unexpected modulation to Amaj7, the first chord of the bridge. This progression is set up in the earlier F9 to G in measures 4–5.

CELEBRATE ME HOME (Kenny Loggins, 1977)

Lyrics by Kenny Loggins
Music by Kenny Loggins and Bob James
© 1977 (Renewed) MILK MONEY MUSIC
All Rights Reserved   Used by Permission

Though this song shows plenty of gospel-style influence, the sophisticated piano part and the man playing them (Bob James) have a jazz pedigree.

The chromatic movement in the inner voice shows deep harmonic sophistication. The harmonies emphasize 7ths, 9ths, and 11ths, and de-emphasize the chord roots. Chord voicings include both note clusters and widely spaced intervals of 4ths and 5ths, generally higher in register and lighter in texture than typical rock voicings. These voicings show a real stylistic difference when compared to chord voicings of other genres covered in this book.

Set as a jazzy swing rhythm, this song has intricate triplet rhythms displaced to different beats. For example, the triplet rhythm is used in a different place in measures 3, 4, and 5: on beat 2, then on beat 1, then on beat 3.

BUTTERFLYZ (Alicia Keys, 2001)

Words and Music by Alicia Keys
© 2001 EMI APRIL MUSIC INC. and LELLOW PRODUCTIONS
All Rights Controlled and Administered by EMI APRIL MUSIC INC.
All Rights Reserved   International Copyright Secured   Used by Permission

The piano is the prominent instrument in Alicia Keys' graceful track, serving as an emotional and textural counterpoint to the lyricism of her vocals.

The left-hand accompaniment supports both the rhythm and harmony by dividing the part between the lowest bass note and the upper chord notes, which are arpeggiated rhythmically. The right-hand part paints a soft, colorful line in a rhythmically syncopated way, but with light, sparse touches that float on top of the left-hand part, tracing a path of circular patterns. The line is shaded with an occasional harmony centered around the major 2nd, in the case of the B and C♯ pairing, and the minor 2nd, in the case of the D♯ and E pairings. The cluster of 2nds culminates in the final measure of the intro, with an F♯ major chord that includes the 4th, 5th, and 6th scale tones played together in a tight cluster.

The following etude focuses on the left-hand techniques used in the song. The movement and rhythm are broken down into distinct parts so you can work to smooth them into a seamless flow.

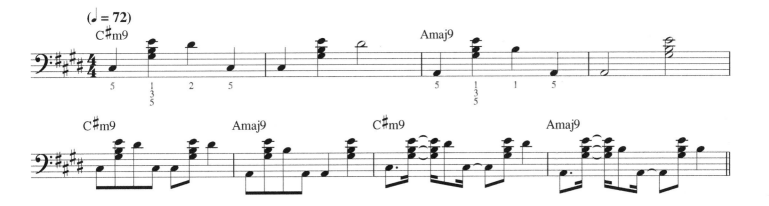

Now incorporate them into the song and add the right-hand part.

I CAN'T MAKE YOU LOVE ME (Bonnie Raitt, 1991)

Words and Music by Mike Reid and Allen Shamblin
Copyright © 1991 ALMO MUSIC CORP., UNIVERSAL MUSIC - MGB SONGS and BRIO BLUES MUSIC
All Rights for BRIO BLUES MUSIC Administered by BMG RIGHTS MANAGEMENT (US) LLC
All Rights Reserved   Used by Permission

One of the most popular songs of the 1990s, and covered by artists across the stylistic spectrum, Bonnie Raitt's classic features gorgeous piano throughout.

Technically speaking, the syncopated left-hand rhythms and 16th note rhythms pose the biggest challenge. To work through and practice these, the exercise below formalizes the rhythmic, melodic, and harmonic elements into patterns so you can master these techniques.

Here is the piano solo that ends the song. It features many jazzy techniques: jazz chords with extensions in clusters; harmonies and melodic lines adorned with copious grace notes and blues notes; off-beats that are emphasized; 32nd-note riffs; and polychords like B♭/E♭ in measures 3 and 6 and E♭/A♭ in measure 10.

★ PART II ★
PIANO SOLOS

ELTON JOHN
Bennie and the Jets (1973)

Elton's iconic piano solo is a fine example of rhythm and blues techniques brought into the pop realm. Elton John started out playing and sounding like a blues man before he created the pop-style megahits with lyricist Bernie Taupin that have come to define his starry career. Those blues influences are evident in this solo in quite a few ways.

The song itself features layered keyboard tracks, with a solo piano track augmenting the main piano track. This solo part is written on the single staff above the grand staff in this transcription. This solo part was piano recorded with reverb effects, giving it the sound of a slightly otherworldly, honky-tonk upright from another place and time.

The signature piano riff is a five-note theme played in octaves on both keyboards. The theme is instantly recognizable and can be considered one of the most famous piano riffs in pop music. The theme traverses the two-chord vamp that defines the harmonic flavor of the song: two parallel major 7th chords played two measures each, and repeated for the intro, transitions, and coda to the song. Somehow this theme captures the satiric edge of the lyric, which both celebrates and mocks the glamorous character types in the music industry.

Measures 1–4 lay out this vamp and precede the start of the solo. In all these measures, the left hand keeps the beat grounded with chord-root octaves played on the beat, written with eighth notes to show the separation between each beat. These separated octaves are like a strobe pulsing through the slow beat of the song. The left-hand octaves are supported by the 5th of the chord, providing a pivot point between the octaves as well as adding to the rhythm. In the right hand, both the Gmaj7 and the Fmaj7 chords move from a straightforward three-note voicing to an alternate. In the case of the Gmaj7, the 5th of the chord, D, moves up to an E and back to a D, coloring the rich sound of the chord with 6ths along with the 7ths. On the Fmaj7, Elton uses a G major triad to move between inversions of the chord in the right-hand voicings. This results in a deeply powerful sound, radiating the F Lydian mode. The left- and right-hand parts combine and complete the syncopated rhythmic patterns, working together to play off the steady quarter-note rhythms of the verses and choruses. This two-handed rhythmic approach continues underneath the piano solo.

The solo starts with a pickup into measure 5 in the single-staff solo part, played by the right hand in treble clef. Rather than outlining the harmonic changes, the solo line works melodically with both the C and G pentatonic scales, and is ornamented with copious grace-note scoops leading chromatically up to the structurally important notes of the melody. These chromatic leading tones culminate in the riff in measure 8, where notes of the E minor triad are preceded by notes a half-step below. Measure 9 continues the solo's peak with clusters of accented and syncopated hits, pushing against the steady four-beat rhythm of the song until it gives way to the tremolo in measure 10.

BILLY JOEL
New York State of Mind (1976)

Billy Joel's bluesy intro to his home-state ode evokes an earlier style, one that features jazzy chords and slow, triplet-based rhythms. It pays musical as well as lyrical tribute to rhythm and blues greats like Ray Charles.

The opening nine measures are made up of mid-range 7th and 9th chords that use the chord arpeggios for riffs and melodic movement. The chords are voiced with octave roots in the left hand and upper chord notes in three- and four-note groupings in the right hand. The piece, in C major, starts on the ii chord, Dm9, and moves to a chord outside the home key, A♭maj7/B♭, in measure 4. This introduces the ♭7th, B♭, one of the blues notes in a C major blues, and sets up the frequent use of other chords built on the ♭7th throughout the song.

With the start of steady tempo in measure 10, the left hand begins a stride-like pattern in half notes, with a single chord root in the low register on beat 1 and an upper triad on beat 3. This establishes the slowly rocking half-time feel that conjures the sound of a slow piano blues. The right-hand part plays a variation of the melody to come later in the verse, over the chord progression used in the verse. The melody is rendered in 3rds, with occasional chromatic runs and filled in with other chord notes. Of particular note are the bluesy turns taken in measures 20 (featuring the ♭3rd, E♭, against the major third, E, in the bass) and 21 (an octave position riff over beats 3 and 4 that outlines the 9th and 13th of the D9 harmony).

Rhythmically, the simple, steady half notes in the left hand allow room for the right hand to play with both a 16th-note feel as well as a triplet feel. Measure 10 is a good example of this, as beat 3 is played with lazy triplets and beat 4 shifts to more urgent 16ths. The quarter-note triplet in measure 18 is soon followed by 16th-note triplets in measures 20 and 21.

Billy uses a near-verbatim transposition of measures 10–12 in measures 14–16, moving from C to the subdominant, F. He uses lots of chord progressions associated with gospel and choral styles – for example the V of IV in measure 13, the V of vi in measure 18, and the V of V in measure 21 and 24. These dominant 7th chords are played in full, strong voicings, perfect for conveying these blues-related styles.

BRUCE HORNSBY
The Way It Is (1986)

The sound of Bruce Hornsby's piano on his biggest hit (see pages 58–59) perfectly captures the spirit of the song's social commentary on economic injustice. The three-note theme is played three times, each time lower in the piano's register. This theme reflects the lyric's lament of the difficulty in overcoming entrenched inequality as well as the strength to stand up to it. The rhythm of the theme is the same each of the three times – two 16th notes followed by a quarter note – but it is placed against the 4/4 beat, lasting two measures, so that it's syncopated.

Before launching into the solo that ends the song, the three-measure theme is played, shown here in measure 1 and held into measure 2. It consists of all five notes of the G pentatonic scale. It starts on the second note of the scale (A), with a G chord underneath, and moves up to the third (B), up to the root (G). This pattern is moved down to start on a G, then starting on a D, while the harmony underneath changes to an F chord, and then a C chord.

Structurally, the 16-measure solo starts on measure 3 and continues through measure 18, using the chord progression of two eight-measure verses. Then the theme is repeated ad lib until the fade out.

Harmonically, the verse chords are all diatonic chords of G major, the chord roots spelling out four of the five notes of the G pentatonic scale. The left-hand part uses open 5ths and octaves to buttress the chord progression, creating a strong foundation to the pentatonic flavor of the solo.

The solo lines in the right hand are also pentatonic in their conception, with nearly all the notes coming from the G pentatonic scale. Part of its appeal is in the way these pentatonic runs, which explore nearly four octaves of the keyboard, roam freely over the four chords. In its way, it reflects a dichotomy that was used in the Romantic era in piano music by Chopin and Liszt, where one element of the composition is constrained while another is given free rein, allowing tension between these opposing elements.

Notable is the way Hornsby uses single-note lines and two- and three-note chord forms to shape the dramatic arc of the solo. It starts with single-note runs, but adds a secondary note at the peak of measure 5, then adds more secondary notes, all pentatonic forms, as the solo builds and ascends the keyboard in measures 8–10, culminating in stronger three-note triads in measures 11 and 12, where the solo reaches its summit.

Ornamenting this acclaimed solo are the many grace notes that are added to the lines and chords, giving the notes they precede a scoop effect, like the articulations of a voice or wind instrument.

BILL PAYNE
Hate to Lose Your Lovin' (1988)

Words and Music by Paul Barrere and Craig Fuller
Copyright © 1988 little feat music (BMI) and feat music (ASCAP)
All Rights Reserved

Bill Payne's solo that leads out of "Hate to Lose Your Lovin'" is a marvel of technical mastery and down-home blues licks. Set over a syncopated pattern straight out of New Orleans-style blues/funk, Payne lets loose dozens of pentatonic riffs, jamming away into the fadeout of the song.

It's important to appreciate the two-measure syncopated pattern that forms the rhythmic basis of the feel here. Take a look at the left-hand part in measures 2 and 3, and then scan through the rest of the left-hand part to see where this pattern and its variations continue, pulling and tugging the rhythm along. If you look back to the earlier chapter on New Orleans Blues, you will find the origins and development of this rhythm pattern.

Now look at the right-hand part in connection with the left-hand part and you see how the two hands work together rhythmically, changing up the syncopations and the rhythm hits as the solo progresses. The two hands fill the gaps in the rhythmic motion: for example, when the left hand plays a note on beat 2 while the right hand has an eighth-note rest in measure 3. Then look at measures 22 and 23, where the hands fill out every eighth note in both measures, but never play at the same time. This alternate-hand style is a big feature of Bill Payne's playing and indicates a percussive approach to the piano that is crucial to rock technique.

Turning to the melodic aspect of the solo, the melody lines and riffs revolve around the D pentatonic and D blues notes. Measure 8 is constructed entirely of the notes of the D pentatonic scale, and melodic riffs using A, B, and D are the most commonly used combinations throughout. C♮ and F♮, the ♭7th and ♭3rd of D major, are found throughout.

The right-hand octave position lines that start the solo are a distinctive feature uses throughout the solo. Payne's right hand is nearly always in an open octave position, performing three different functions: playing a melodic line in octaves (measures 14 and 15); playing an octave hit with either a 4th or 5th in between for support and strength (the last chord of measure 8 and the first chord of measure 9); or surrounding a melodic line that occurs in between the octaves. This last function is the most unique, and can be seen right away in measures 2 and 3. The octave As surround the actual melodic line of the solo: the middle voice. Play that middle voice without the octave As and you'll clearly hear the melodic line come through. See how this continues in measures 4 and 5, and is used at various points throughout the solo.

Other noteworthy techniques are the tremolo chord in measure 3, the bluesy grace-note scoops at the beginning of measures 7 and 14, and the string of 3rds in the right hand from measure 23 through 26.

Bill Payne's solo takes command of the entire keyboard, an excellent example of virtuoso improvising in a bluesy rock setting.

RICHARD TEE
Gone at Last (1975)

In the solo that ends the Paul Simon hit, Richard Tee uses classic gospel piano techniques to give the song its hallelujah spirit. (See page 64.) His blues licks are harmonized with church chords and his rhythms are strong and syncopated.

The rhythmic grounding of the song is found in the left-hand part. Steady quarter notes that alternate between the root and 5th of each chord keep the beat steady and anchor the syncopated right-hand rhythms in a 4/4 framework. You can see how his right-hand rhythms emphasize the offbeats all the way through the solo, either landing on the eighth or 16ths between beats. His phrases end on syncopated beats, like the last eighth of the bar in measures 1, 2, and 3, or the eighth before beat 3 as in measures 6, 8, 12, 14, and 16.

The chord progression is simple – it doesn't wander far from the C major/A minor context, changing from an A minor to C7 to F and back to C7. The C7 is the I chord, with the 7th reflecting the blues scale rather than as a dominant resolving to F.

The right-hand melodic line traces notes in the C major scale, with added notes from the C blues scale: the ♭7th (B♭), ♭5th (G♭ or F♯), and the ♭3rd (E♭). What puts the solo in the gospel style is the harmonization of the line with triads and octave chords, a technique that stays consistent throughout. This harmonization shows a great deal of inventive passing chord technique that is rooted in choral style – blocks of sound moving smoothly through a hymn or phrases of a gospel shout. Passing chords he uses off the A minor include G major, E♭ major, and C minor. From the C7, Tee uses F major, F minor, D minor, as well as C diminished and C minor to harmonize the melodic lines. And from the F major, Tee employs C minor and D minor triads with the melodic lines. He utilizes the C diminished chord to resolve up to a C major chord, so that the diminished tones (the 3rd and the 5th) are always moving a half step up to the natural 3rd and natural 5th, in measures 7, 11, 12, and 15.

It's impressive to see how little ornamentation Tee wields, and how little in the way of the flashier techniques like glissandos or tremolos. Instead, the beauty of his solo is in the harmonic play, when a simple line over a C7 chord can be harmonized with four different passing chords, as in measure 7.

SARA BAREILLES

Gravity (2009)

Sara Bareilles uses the piano to paint the emotional undercurrents of her ballad, and this transcription of the chorus shows exactly how she does it. (See page 66.) The ambivalent forces of the lyric are registered in subtle ways; given the sparseness of the accompaniment, each dynamic nuance and each added chord tone takes on significance.

The main ingredient of contrast here is the use of closely voiced harmonic clusters followed by larger, open intervals. In measure 1, the chord on beat 1 uses only the most potent of the chord tones – the 7th under the 3rd topped by the 4th of a D minor chord. But in the balance of the measure, only the outer notes of the voicing are used, and the open 5th sound of the C and G over a D bass suddenly clears away the richness of the clustered 3rd and 4th and creates the haunting mood of a chord in stasis.

Another ingredient of contrast is the opposition of the single-note bass line to the clustered harmonies in the right. The melodic movement of the bass line is simple and clear, while the right-hand chords are more ambiguous.

This shows the importance of detail needed to bring out the shadings and contrasts of Bareilles's style. In measures 3 and 4, the same factors are at work. In the left hand, a single-note bass line moves down scalewise from C to G, using syncopations before beat 3 in both measures. In the right hand, the clustered seconds appear in three different chords as the lower notes of each voicing before opening up into a triad moved to a register an octave higher. The clusters create subtle but noticeable dissonance with the bass notes until the A minor triad clears the sound into a light, transparent harmony, hovering again in stasis above a non-chordal G in the bass.

The four-measure chord progression is repeated in measures 5–8, culminating in the most unusual harmony of the song: an Fmaj9/A. This inverted voicing brings the contrasting elements together in a polychord, with a C major triad in the right hand over an inverted F chord in the left, and the cluster in the middle where the G meets the F.

Measures 10 and 11 show how carefully Bareilles uses notes outside the basic triad to give color and shading to her piano parts. The perfect 5th in the left hand of measure 10 gives a clear feeling of B♭ major, and indicates a move away from the simple C major tonality of the song. Yet in the right hand she plays the 6th (G) and 9th (C) of the B♭ chord, again creating a two-note cluster in the middle of the voicing. And because the chord doesn't have a D, the major 3rd, it adds to the ambiguity of the harmony, rather like a painter who creates colors neither light nor dark, but something containing elements of each.

KEITH EMERSON
Trilogy (1972)

Music by Keith Emerson and Greg Lake
Copyright © 1972 (Renewed) Leadchoice Ltd.
Administered Worldwide by Campbell & Co. Ltd.
International Copyright Secured   All Rights Reserved
Reprinted by Permission of Music Sales Corporation

The stylistic features in this virtuosic solo are found in much of the music of Emerson, Lake and Palmer, and distinguish it by ambitiously combining rock and European classical music. Emerson based his approach on the styles and techniques of Romantic composers like Rachmaninoff, Chopin, and Liszt. He was fearless in pushing the boundaries of rock to embrace a broader musical language.

The overall approach here is juxtaposition: lyrical themes are juxtaposed with biting harmonies; smooth arpeggios are juxtaposed with accented chords; 4/4 meters are juxtaposed with three- and five-beat meters; a triad in one measure is juxtaposed with a chord built in 4ths in another. This not only sounds very cool in a rock setting, it expands the vocabulary of rock to the level of a tone poem, as the music takes a prominent role in describing and illustrating the emotions of a song.

We get the first look at juxtaposition in measure 1, which leads into the extended solo. (See page 68.) The F♯ harmonies of beat 1 are quickly erased with the unrelated and alternating D major and A minor triads, voiced in thick block chords that march down the keyboard like a Rachmaninoff piano concerto. In measure 2 we are back in B major, with a theme derived from the chord notes. In beats 3 and 4, the right-hand line takes the theme to the dominant (F♯), while the left hand moves to the subdominant (E), in the first of many polychords – a juxtaposition of one chord over another. Using the technique of harmonic development, Emerson takes the polychord through a series of descending whole-step transpositions in measure 4, resolving them to B major in measure 5. Measures 7 and 8 bring back the opening theme of the song in the right hand, working with the juxtaposition of B major and G major and developing it though measure 17. Here the progression is transformed into a juxtaposition of B major and F♯ minor, finally giving way to F major in measure 22, where the tonal pull of B major has given way to a new section, where harmony moves freely between unrelated chords.

This new section is a rhapsodic exploration of B major harmonies juxtaposed with sonorities drawn from a completely unrelated tonality: F Lydian. This is about as far apart as you can get, harmonically speaking, and Emerson explores the possible harmonies in ways that suggest an epic quest – quite a grandiose and romantic concept.

Changes of meter, changes of register, and virtuosic passagework are found in abundance in this section, with a field day of techniques like arpeggios, etude-like patterns, and contrasting 16th and triplet rhythms.

The solo ends with a rhythmic vamp in 5/4 meter, a relatively new and rare feature of rock at the time it was written, that juxtaposes B♭ major and B/F harmonies in jarring, uneven patterns, kicks the song into high gear, and puts the conflicting harmonies to work musically illustrating the conflict at the heart of the songs lyric.

Good - bye, _____

good - bye. _____

ABOUT THE AUTHOR

The author of *Piano Exercises for Dummies, The Art of Billy Strayhorn, The Art of Steely Dan,* and *Color Your Chords,* **David Pearl** arranged *The Jazz Piano Collection,* 22 jazz standards for solo piano, and *Bach 'n' Roll,* 20 pop songs set in the styles of the great classical composers, along with numerous other music books published by Cherry Lane Music and Music Sales Corporation. He recently co-authored *100 Blues Lessons* for Hal Leonard's Keyboard Lesson Goldmine Series. His other books include jazz transcriptions of the artists Grover Washington Jr., Dave Douglas, Roland Hanna, and Wynton Marsalis. Born in Denver, Colorado, he graduated from the Lamont School of Music at the University of Denver, and lives in New York City, where he keeps busy performing, arranging, and composing.

KEYBOARD STYLE SERIES

THE COMPLETE GUIDE!

These book/audio packs provide focused lessons that contain valuable how-to insight, essential playing tips, and beneficial information for all players. From comping to soloing, comprehensive treatment is given to each subject. The companion audio features many of the examples in the book performed either solo or with a full band.

BEBOP JAZZ PIANO
by John Valerio

This book provides detailed information for bebop and jazz keyboardists on: chords and voicings, harmony and chord progressions, scales and tonality, common melodic figures and patterns, comping, characteristic tunes, the styles of Bud Powell and Thelonious Monk, and more.
00290535 Book/Online Audio $18.99

BEGINNING ROCK KEYBOARD
by Mark Harrison

This comprehensive book/audio package will teach you the basic skills needed to play beginning rock keyboard. From comping to soloing, you'll learn the theory, the tools, and the techniques used by the pros. The accompanying audio demonstrates most of the music examples in the book.
00311922 Book/Online Audio $14.99

BLUES PIANO
by Mark Harrison

With this book/audio pack, you'll learn the theory, the tools, and even the tricks that the pros use to play the blues. Covers: scales and chords; left-hand patterns; walking bass; endings and turnarounds; right-hand techniques; how to solo with blues scales; crossover licks; and more.
00311007 Book/Online Audio $19.99

BOOGIE-WOOGIE PIANO
by Todd Lowry

From learning the basic chord progressions to inventing your own melodic riffs, you'll learn the theory, tools and techniques used by the genre's best practicioners.
00117067 Book/Online Audio $17.99

BRAZILIAN PIANO
by Robert Willey and Alfredo Cardim

Brazilian Piano teaches elements of some of the most appealing Brazilian musical styles: choro, samba, and bossa nova. It starts with rhythmic training to develop the fundamental groove of Brazilian music.
00311469 Book/Online Audio $19.99

CONTEMPORARY JAZZ PIANO
by Mark Harrison

From comping to soloing, you'll learn the theory, the tools, and the techniques used by the pros. The full band tracks on the audio feature the rhythm section on the left channel and the piano on the right channel, so that you can play along with the band.
00311848 Book/Online Audio $18.99

COUNTRY PIANO
by Mark Harrison

Learn the theory, the tools, and the tricks used by the pros to get that authentic country sound. This book/audio pack covers: scales and chords, walkup and walkdown patterns, comping in traditional and modern country, Nashville "fretted piano" techniques and more.
00311052 Book/Online Audio $19.99

GOSPEL PIANO
by Kurt Cowling

Discover the tools you need to play in a variety of authentic gospel styles, through a study of rhythmic devices, grooves, melodic and harmonic techniques, and formal design. The accompanying audio features over 90 tracks, including piano examples as well as the full gospel band.
00311327 Book/Online Adio $17.99

INTRO TO JAZZ PIANO
by Mark Harrison

From comping to soloing, you'll learn the theory, the tools, and the techniques used by the pros. The accompanying audio demonstrates most of the music examples in the book. The full band tracks feature the rhythm section on the left channel and the piano on the right channel, so that you can play along with the band.
00312088 Book/Online Audio $17.99

JAZZ-BLUES PIANO
by Mark Harrison

This comprehensive book will teach you the basic skills needed to play jazz-blues piano. Topics covered include: scales and chords • harmony and voicings • progressions and comping • melodies and soloing • characteristic stylings.
00311243 Book/Online Audio $17.99

JAZZ-ROCK KEYBOARD
by T. Lavitz

Learn what goes into mixing the power and drive of rock music with the artistic elements of jazz improvisation in this comprehensive book and CD package. This instructional tool delves into scales and modes, and how they can be used with various chord progressions to develop the best in soloing chops.
00290536 Book/CD Pack...$17.95

LATIN JAZZ PIANO
by John Valerio

This book is divided into three sections. The first covers Afro-Cuban (Afro-Caribbean) jazz, the second section deals with Brazilian influenced jazz – Bossa Nova and Samba, and the third contains lead sheets of the tunes and instructions for the play-along audio.
00311345 Book/Online Audio $17.99

MODERN POP KEYBOARD
by Mark Harrison

From chordal comping to arpeggios and ostinatos, from grand piano to synth pads, you'll learn the theory, the tools, and the techniques used by the pros. The online audio demonstrates most of the music examples in the book.
00146596 Book/Online Audio $17.99

NEW AGE PIANO
by Todd Lowry

From melodic development to chord progressions to left-hand accompaniment patterns, you'll learn the theory, the tools and the techniques used by the pros. The accompanying 96-track CD demonstrates most of the music examples in the book.
00117322 Book/CD Pack...$16.99

HAL•LEONARD®

Prices, contents, and availability
subject to change without notice.

www.halleonard.com

POST-BOP JAZZ PIANO
by John Valerio

This book/audio pack will teach you the basic skills needed to play post-bop jazz piano. Learn the theory, the tools, and the tricks used by the pros to play in the style of Bill Evans, Thelonious Monk, Herbie Hancock, McCoy Tyner, Chick Corea and others. Topics covered include: chord voicings, scales and tonality, modality, and more.
00311005 Book/Online Audio $17.99

PROGRESSIVE ROCK KEYBOARD
by Dan Maske

You'll learn how soloing techniques, form, rhythmic and metrical devices, harmony, and counterpoint all come together to make this style of rock the unique and exciting genre it is.
00311307 Book/Online Audio $19.99

R&B KEYBOARD
by Mark Harrison

From soul to funk to disco to pop, you'll learn the theory, the tools, and the tricks used by the pros with this book/audio pack. Topics covered include: scales and chords, harmony and voicings, progressions and comping, rhythmic concepts, characteristic stylings, the development of R&B, and more! Includes seven songs.
00310881 Book/Online Audio $19.99

ROCK KEYBOARD
by Scott Miller

Learn to comp or solo in any of your favorite rock styles. Listen to the audio to hear your parts fit in with the total groove of the band. Includes 99 tracks! Covers: classic rock, pop/rock, blues rock, Southern rock, hard rock, progressive rock, alternative rock and heavy metal.
00310823 Book/Online Audio $17.99

ROCK 'N' ROLL PIANO
by Andy Vinter

Take your place alongside Fats Domino, Jerry Lee Lewis, Little Richard, and other legendary players of the '50s and '60s! This book/audio pack covers: left-hand patterns; basic rock 'n' roll progressions; right-hand techniques; straight eighths vs. swing eighths; glisses, crushed notes, rolls, note clusters and more. Includes six complete tunes.
00310912 Book/Online Audio $18.99

SALSA PIANO
by Hector Martignon

From traditional Cuban music to the more modern Puerto Rican and New York styles, you'll learn the all-important rhythmic patterns of salsa and how to apply them to the piano. The book provides historical, geographical and cultural background info, and the 50+-tracks includes piano examples and a full salsa band percussion section.
00311049 Book/Online Audio $19.99

SMOOTH JAZZ PIANO
by Mark Harrison

Learn the skills you need to play smooth jazz piano – the theory, the tools, and the tricks used by the pros. Topics covered include: scales and chords; harmony and voicings; progressions and comping; rhythmic concepts; melodies and soloing; characteristic stylings; discussions on jazz evolution.
00311095 Book/Online Audio $19.99

STRIDE & SWING PIANO
by John Valerio

Learn the styles of the stride and swing piano masters, such as Scott Joplin, Jimmy Yancey, Pete Johnson, Jelly Roll Morton, James P. Johnson, Fats Waller, Teddy Wilson, and Art Tatum. This book/audio pack covers classic ragtime, early blues and boogie woogie, New Orleans jazz and more. Includes 14 songs.
00310882 Book/Online Audio $19.99

WORSHIP PIANO
by Bob Kauflin

From chord inversions to color tones, from rhythmic patterns to the Nashville Numbering System, you'll learn the tools and techniques needed to play piano or keyboard in a modern worship setting.
00311425 Book/Online Audio $17.99